LET'S START!

fantastic!

yippee!

cheer up!

wonderful!

ready,
set,
go!

stay strong!

love blooms!

grand
Slam!

help others!

shine
bright!

hooray!

hit a home run!

let's
get
moving!

art
science
math
study
hard!

love yourself!

aim
high!
01

the best

stop and smell the flowers!

take the lead!

enjoy
the little
things!

1st

make
today
magical!

SUPER!

you
rock

Made in United States
Orlando, FL
09 September 2024

51302844R00028